A LEGACY OF LYRICS

A LEGACY OF LYRICS

By

FLORENCE HESTER EDGAR

TORONTO

THE UNIVERSITY OF TORONTO PRESS

1946

FLORENCE HESTER EDGAR, 1908

FOREWORD

THE AUTHOR of the following poems was born some seventy odd years ago in the village of Dundrum, a suburb of Dublin, Ireland, near the picturesque Dublin hills and the Irish Channel. Her father was William Andrew Hayes, a prosperous merchant and landowner. Her mother, Mary Eleanor Pratt Hayes, came of a well-known family of County Cavan. To finish her education she spent some years at a school in Germany, where she became proficient in the French and German languages. While still abroad she was called home owing to the serious illness of her father, who died soon after her return. The next year, she travelled to the United States with her mother and three sisters, going as far as Chicago. There, for two or three years, she gave private lessons in languages, and then with mother and sisters returned to Ireland.

In 1900, when visiting Arromanches, a small fishing town on the coast of Normandy, she met Mrs. Dale Harris of Ottawa, with whom she came to Canada at the end of the summer. In 1903, in the suburb of Isleworth, near London, she was married to William Wilkie Edgar, son of the late Sir James Edgar of Toronto. From that time she had lived in Ottawa, until her sudden passing, on March 31, 1944.

In 1908, she earned distinction as an actress through winning a gold bracelet offered by Miss Margaret Anglin, a Canadian who for many years had been prominent on the American stage. This prize was awarded to the best actress in the Earl Grey Dramatic Trophy Competition, won by the Ottawa Thespian Club largely through her brilliant acting in "The Light of Saint Agnes," a beautiful one-act tragedy. Great versatility was also shown by her acting as a comedienne in "Food and Folly," an original farce, offered by her club on the same occasion.

After her decease, there was found among her effects a quantity of compositions in prose and verse almost ready for publication. From this literary bequest has been selected the poetry that follows. Some poems have already appeared in the daily press of Ottawa, and others in a small brochure brought out a few years ago. But most of the poems are now offered to the reading public for the first time, and the editor bespeaks for them a cordial reception.

The editor wishes to express here his sincere thanks to his friend, Dr. Duncan Campbell Scott, and to his brother, Dr. Pelham Edgar, for their great aid in the work of selecting and editing, and in the preparation of the book for the printer.

W. W. E.

CONTENTS

THOUGHTS ON BOOKS

Books are my silent friends and true:
And when I seek within their hidden store
For vaster knowledge and for ancient lore,
The gifted thoughts transcribed by pen,
The harvest rare of other men,
Before me and beyond, the wider sphere
Draws back the curtain of the passing year.

ALETHEA

(A legend of ancient Greece)

THE youth, Phileron, wrought in plastic
     clay,
And sought the perfect touch of Grecian art
While dark-eyed Alethea left her play
To pose for him, who held her dear at heart.

His 'prentice days passed like the glinting
     beams
Of sun, that brighten cliffs, and sky, and sea.
His triumphs, hopes and fears, ambitions,
     dreams,
He shared with her, who was his bride to be.

But rapture such as theirs may scarce endure
While gods their human jealousies display.
Bright Alethea sees sweet life's allure
Grow dim, as Pluto snatches her away.

The Fates snap short the thread, relentlessly,
Of her gay life, and now, with icy dread,
She sips love's proffered chalice wearily,
Since all her tender hopes and dreams are
     fled.

With anguished soul Phileron roams the
    glades,
The fairest flowers for him have lost all charm,
Sea storms re-echo moans of Pluto's shades:
His lovely bride—why should she come to
    harm!

He thought of Orpheus, who nearly brought
Eurydice from Hades by his art,
And of Pygmalion, who deftly wrought
His Galatea, seeking to impart

Life's spark, whereby she smiled and moved
    and spoke.
Was his, Phileron's, love less stout and
    strong
To strive for Alethea? If she woke,
He'd win her back to life from Pluto's
    throng:

The gods might deign to work the miracle!
To Delphi he repairs with broken heart:
To his appeal outspake the Oracle:
"Learn from the winged brothers of thine
    art."

He fails to read the Delphic riddle right,
And puzzles o'er the answer every day,
Until in spring two mating birds alight
Within the pit where he must dig his clay.

From this same clay he sees them build
    their nest,
And shape with bills, then line it warm and
    soft.
"These are my winged brothers, no god's
    jest
That Oracle, but wisdom from aloft."

A happy silence reigns, the eggs are laid,
They wait in brooding, hushed expectancy,
Until their little house of clay is made
Full of life's gift to their sweet constancy.

At last the cryptic key for which he yearns
Is manifest, as slowly there awakes
Love for his feathered friends, from whom
    he learns
New lessons as the nesting silence breaks.

The parents' watchful ministry above,
The careful nursing of the mother bird,
Their tireless flights for food, their pride and
    love,
The eager chirps of fledgelings often heard

He notes, and on the day the young take
      wing,
He sees them poised uncertain, held by fear,
And then fly forth. His heart with joy can
      sing
In unison with parents hovering near.

"Ye feathered folk that wing your trackless
      way
Across the oceans to some sun-kissed clime,
Ye bear a message from the gods to say
Where love and beauty call in their due
      time!"

Once more his soul with melody is filled,
He sees his true love tripping through the
      glades,
'Mid flowers and trees where fragrance is
      distilled,
His Alethea mingling with their shades.

Quickly Phileron takes his tools once more,
And moulds in clay his loved one's dainty
      charms,
Nor will he pause for aught, nor rest, before
His art has rounded out the lovely arms,

The pulsing throat and all the witching
grace.
With throbbing heart he kneels as darkness
falls;
Enshrouded in the mists he sees her face,
And on Love's mother, Aphrodite, calls.

Without the casement shines a golden light;
He turns, and there beside the risen moon,
Behold the Queen of Love, whose tones de-
light:
"For thy devotion I will grant a boon."

The homing swallows circle round her head.
One lights upon her lily hand upraised.
"By this swift messenger thy bride is led.
Farewell!" Alone Phileron stands, amazed.

Where in the dark his lost bride's figure
stands,
Seeing a moonbeam kiss her waving hair,
Phileron cries, with outstretched pleading
hands,
"Awake to life! The gods have heard my
prayer."

She stirs, she speaks, she smiles with love-lit
      eyes,
And once again he folds her in his arms.
"Forever thus, my love!" But Death denies
A joy so great: and with morn's first alarms,

"Back to my dark abode," saith she, "I go,
Where on the Queen Persephone I wait.
By this swift swallow's feather, thou mayest
      know
My love endures, be not disconsolate!"

The swallow on her wrist with open wings
Strains at his leash, impatient for the flight;
She holds the bird with gauzy, silken strings,
As they sail forth beneath the dawn's first
      light.

In joy Phileron plies his art, and hopes
The day may come when love will conquer
      all,
And with his mortal tasks he bravely copes,
While o'er the sea floats Alethea's call.

MARCH ON

Again, the web of stirring life
Beneath a canopy of snow,
A stormy March has waged his strife
Yet left no mark of lasting woe.

In skies, the dawn's bright living flame
A glory made of rose and mauve,
To honour thus a Holy Name
And, interchanging, wrought and wove

A tale that men must ever tell
When harmony and beauty meet
To link the dead past with "all's well!"
While glad Earth rises, both to greet.

Her coil of seasons onward spins
With lavish gifts to aid the race:
In every clime Dame Nature wins,
Her bounty spreads with saving grace.

Though watchers see the darkness fade
And Earth in robes of snowy white,
Yet, strong in purpose, plans are laid,
Victorious life still wins the fight.

THE AFTERMATH

THERE are storms of earth, air, sea, of single souls and of a multitude of souls swayed by one impulse. Who will ever forget a tossing in the trough of an angry sea; or roaring mountainous billows rushing shoreward only to break and retreat, obeying the Divine command: "Thus far!"; or the awe caused by a high wind racing through a forest, uprooting giants in its path; or driving in a deluge of rain, suggesting a revocation of the promise: "No more flood," to the accompaniment of crashing thunder and flashing lightning! The succession of rapid changes made memorable a storm which broke over Ottawa on March 17, 1934. Nature, in many moods, proved her power to destroy utterly, or to soothe tired humanity into a semblance of peace, prepared to carry on their work in Creation's plan. Man seldom gives a thought to the influences guiding his destiny, or to the awful power which natural forces if released might exercise, to eclipse or further his puny schemes. The unseen hand moves on, tendering healing loveliness to those who daily stand on the threshold of life and death, that they may sip and find tranquillity therein.

THE CHALICE

How strange the night! But first, of such a
    night
And all it would reveal.   Within a room
Devoid of furnishings, except for need,
A form inanimate, death's counterfeit.
It seemed as if the spirit kept a tryst
Beyond.   The lonely watcher knew that
    Death,
The enemy, was near, just held at bay
By   gentlest   ministerings   and   pleading
    prayer
That winged for healing meed to Heaven's
    gate.
Then sudden dark clouds broke in clashing
    din.
A peal of mighty thunder rolled, and shook
The vivid skies with darts of lightning riven.
Torrential   rain   of   sleet   like   flood-gates
    loosed
Descended, deluging the frozen Earth,
And held her bound and chained in clear,
    cold ice.

Each creature fled to cover. Silence reigned,
Profound and strange. The arch foe fled,
    in fear
He too might be a prisoner, till the trump
Resound to call the dead, and overthrow
Man's last great enemy.
                            Anon, fair dawn
Came tenderly in pearls and fleecy clouds.
The watcher, heavenward gazing, saw with
    awe
A beauty leaving naught to be desired.
There, riding quite alone with Venus close,
The Queen of Night in most majestic poise
An upward crescent like a vessel formed,
With lip and handle curious, wrought and
    chased,
Surpassing all perfection's skill hereto
Attained in craftsmanship—a heavenly
    cup!
With how sublime a comeliness she rode!
As conscious of a new-found dignity,
Ordained to bring to pass divine events.
A goblet filled and tendered to the stars,
That sipped the molten gold and soft with-
    drew.
Alone in that vast wind-swept vault above,
With her attendant, Venus, radiant, white,

A Queen of Dawn in beauty unexcelled,
She filled the soul with sweet content and
    hope,
And brought the exhausted body ease. She
    breathed
Of nobler missions foreign to our Earth,
Of planes of thought to lift mankind from
    dross.
The twain in rapt communion vigil kept,
As if to celebrate some ancient rite,
Commingling thoughts of high resolve and
    love,
As knights of old, who ventured on a quest
To seek the *Holy Grail*, long lost to man.
    A solemn silence reigned, a healing balm,
The Earth with every leaflet coated fast
So glistening white and like a sea of glass,
The Sky a tribute to her lovely Queen
With Venus gentlest of the morning stars.
The soul perceives with deeper conscious-
    ness
The revelation of that firmament,
In peace surpassing comprehension here,
And sips as thirsty stars had sipped the pure
Bright mead from that strange chalice,
    flowing free.

How great a gift! How marvellous a prize!
   Then, through the silence that succeeds
     a storm
Of thunder wind and fire and rain and stress,
A still voice floated down to cheer and thrill,
And comfort like enfolding angels' wings:
"Drink, thirsty one, and live! *I am* hath
   sent
The *Holy Grail* men lost their lives to win.
This mead will give surcease from pain."
   Thus passed
The vision of the *Holy Grail*, but left
An impress on the mind that viewed the cup
And drained the liquid, warm and comfort-
   ing,
While Dawn rose blushingly to gladden
   Earth.
   In due time burst the Sun upon the
   scene,
Transforming festooned icicles and seas
Of glass to glowing jewels without price.
He clothed the Earth in raiment that out-
   shone
Man's chiefest treasures, prized for purity.
Such changes followed in this wake of storm:
Enraptured Nature saw her vast domain
So exquisite none dared behold it quite.

A pæan of praise and gratitude went forth
From every littlest blade and bush and tree
That sparkled in their coats of mail. On
    wires
Hung glittering pendants over ways and
    fields,
With pageantry of swiftly changing lights.
    Days passed while peace endured, Earth
    seemed to pause
And cease from toil of meeting human needs.
Deep in the hush a still small voice pre-
    vailed,
Prophetic whisperings through the troubled
    years:
"I am that I am--the Way, the Truth, the Life.
Ho! Everyone that thirsteth, drink and live!"

LIGHT DAWNS

O TROUBLED heart be still!
Your crystal deeps
May garner warm sun rays
For treasure,
And diffusing them from every facet
Flash them forth in beauty, strength and
    colour.

As sunbeams break and scatter
A hopeless day's dull mists,
Harmonious thoughts, fleet-winged,
Are swift to clear the soul's despondent
    skies,
Wind-swept by storms of stress,
Gleanings of drifting clouds.

From Winter's reign of ice
Emerges a people's soul,
Quick with homage and yearning
As the first glad breath of Spring
Draws away the slime and anguish,
Fulfilling God's promise to Earth.

Awake and sing, my love,
In unison with those effulgent rays!
They draw chill frost from trees
And melt soiled snow to vapour.
So cast away all cares!
In darkest woods light dawns.

WE ARE LABOURERS TOGETHER WITH GOD

(After a radio sermon, in March, 1938, based on a text from I Corinthians 2:9)

WE all are labourers with God,
Who calls us to His harvesting,
To turn with Him the well-worn sod,
And place within the soil a seed.

O, bless Thy Kingdom with increase,
Which we together share with Thee!
Our plot of life from Thee we lease,
And dare not let it vacant lie.

Come, fostering sunshine, wind and rain,
On all our work in secret there,
That we may see the tender grain
Shoot forth and cover this good earth!

The people, sure of Thy goodwill,
Give thanks to Thee with one accord,
For gifts of time and urge and skill,
To work in concord with Thy law.

SHEPHERDS ALL

SHEPHERDS haste your flocks to keep!
Speed through fields where they may
    sleep,
In the snow and rain and murk,
Where the hungry wild wolves lurk.

Follow them, oh, follow on!
Till you know where each has gone.
Call the lambkins by their name,
Seek the lost one, lone and lame!

Search the coverts, find the stray!
Stars of hope will point the way.
In warm arms enfold it fast,
Safe from dangers quickly passed.

Follow them, oh, follow on!
Lest all little lambs be gone.
Hear them answer to your call!
Kindly Love will gather all.

CHRISTMAS IN MERRIE ENGLAND

It's ever Merrie England when Christmas
    draweth nigh,
The folks pack up their troubles and sorrows
    are put by,
They wonder if, this year, with many shakes
    and nods,
It will be white or green. Now, tell us,
    what's the odds?

The kiddies watch for Santa's fleetest of
    reindeer,
His load of things from toyland and harvest
    of good cheer,
While many jolly mummers will carol
    through the land
With free for all a welcome to make the
    heart expand.

Oh, well we know the reason for this quaint-
    est old-world rite
That follows down the ages to celebrate this
    night,
And blend with sacred feelings in melodies
    of tone
The ties that bind Old England, set in the
    sea alone.

CHRISTMAS PEACE

O GOD, that gavest purity and love,
To guide us through the perils of this life
And make the world a very haven of peace,
Give us the will to prize the things above!

Why do men strive in lust and murderous
    hate?
Like filthy refuse in a gathered heap
Malicious thoughts will rise in deadly fumes
To choke the race and leave it desolate.

In Hell's despite, humanity must grow
In nobleness, and wield the gracious powers
Bestowed divinely, with intent to raise
Mankind, not cast him to a cruel foe.

As Satan and his hosts were hurled away
When black rebellion shook the gates of
    Heaven,
So every soul that hears not love's appeal
Fades out, if he observe not Christmas Day.

The birthday of a glorious Child of old
Is still the birth of noble deeds and love,
So raise the standard for the Child's sweet
    sake,
Until stands Everyman for peace enrolled.

TWO BABES

There are two babes, whose glowing words
    and deeds
Have graced the page of history down the
    years;
The twain had perished at a tyrant's word,
Save only mother love foresaw the doom
And swiftly hid the babes away, until
The dreaded peril passed. One, in an ark
Among the flags beside the river's brink,
Touched Pharaoh's daughter with a piteous
    cry,
And woke in her compassion kin to love.
Full grown, this babe brake Israel's bonds
    and led
The people through the sea to fertile lands.
He wrote in stone the Ten Commands that
    rule
Our conduct to this very day. They pass
Unheeded by the multitude, but still
A remnant keep these mystic words of God.

There came in low estate the Infant Christ,
Ordained of royal David's line a king,
Whom cruel Herod ruthlessly had slain
But that His parents fled. This Babe when
    grown

Fulfilled the law, and set the spirit free
To love the Lord Creator first, and next
His neighbour as himself, and live in peace.
Thus had the doors of strife been closed,
    but once
Again unheeded, all these loving words
Are lost in surging hate and rivalry.
Still, round the season of His birthday feast,
That Babe's sweet presence softens every
    heart.
The glory of His song inspires the host,
And all the gracious fruits of Earth arise
To gladden life and fill the hungry soul.

THE DIVINE GARDENER

Snow blossoms clustered on the trees that
  day,
At Easter dawn, when people rose to pray,
The ninth of April found the ground so
  white,
Suffused by Resurrection's holy light;

The petals, frail as those the angels spray
When calling happy children forth to play,
Or giving men a feast of manna pure,
A tender feast of love, their griefs to cure.

For all who glimpsed His resurrected Might
Dispel the darkness by dawn's rosy light
Saw beauty fill the world with harmony,
And bring to mourning souls new rhapsody,

Like Mary's, when she asked the gardener
  where
Her vanished Lord might be—Lo! He
  stood there!
"Rabboni, Master! Come the world to
  save!
Thy glories stretch beyond an earthly
  grave."

THE GIFT ETERNAL

OUT of the mists a Voice rising and falling
Wakes the abyss where life answers the
    calling,
Spanning new distance in time and vast
    space.
Instinct with love a still form is moving,
Vitalized energy growing in grace,
Following pathways that starcraft is groov-
    ing
Earthwards, for life's full completion un-
    folding.
Skyward reflected, a glittering molding,
Round him the universe flashing in light,
Radiant sunshine brightening the day,
Silvery moonbeams illumining night,
Star-clusters gathering in splendid array.
Laden with scent burst the blossoming
    trees,
Vocal with carolling birds' melodies,
Fruits in their season are bending down low,
Pure waters gurgling in merriment flow,
Soft breezes' whispering harmonies blend,
Fragrance and colourings sweet flowers lend.
Earth quick with increase delivers her yield,
Dowering her finest, true prowess to shield.

All with a purpose in Nature's grand scheme,
Fusing the perfect to make life supreme.
Great with emotion her lord begins reaping
Beauties and wealth without limit or keep-
    ing,
Tendering his praise to the Spirit bestowing
Treasures on Cosmos, unceasingly growing.
Life, the great gift, sends him wisdom for
    gleaning
Mysteries perplexing with infinite meaning.

CAELI ENARRANT

(Thoughts from Psalm 19)

Caeli enarrant the glory of God!
From the uttermost parts of Heaven this
     song
Rises in cadence, a wonderful voice,
Chanting to people, deep and strong.

Caeli enarrant the sun's great course!
Like a bridegroom rejoicing to honour his
     bride,
In joy he speeds to the ends of the world,
Trooping his colours with giant's pride.

One day telleth another the law
Of time and space in its circuit unbound,
One night whispers the other's soft light
Secrets the moon and the stars have found.

Caeli enarrant the statutes of God
Proven and best for the race of man,
Harmonies shaping His handiwork
Changeless of purpose since they began.

WINGED SECRETS

PANDORA's box is filled with things,
Such lovely things with gauzy wings!
But if you lift the lid, they'll fly
Where none may guess, they soar so high.

Within this magic box are dreams,
Oh quite invisible it seems.
A girl may glimpse the bravest boy,
The guardian of her life's full joy.

The boy may see her lovely face,
Just wreathed in smiles and witching grace.
Now, close that lock and take the key,
And keep the secrets! None should see

Those dainty things Hope holds in there,
A host you can't with others share,
They add the little spice of life,
The wings to mount above Earth's strife.

ON A SUNDIAL

THE finger of a god points here:
While Time rolls back the fleeting hour
And night descending drops a veil,
The hand unseen moves slowly on,
Untiring in the task that's set.
Awakening dawn to us reveals
The warning finger's beacon sign,
While our own task is still undone.

WINGS

THE world is scarce a toy to idly spin
With matter sating man with earthly
    things,
If mystic powers of mind at last begin
To triumph, he may rise on magic wings.

THE RACE

How shall we run the race that's set
Without a hindrance or a let,
And steer a course through life's high sea
That leads to paths of victory?

The many ways at length converge
Where Everyman must soon emerge,
Through pastures green he wanders on
With rod and staff to lean upon.

The gate is open as he nears,
And Love in human form appears;
Soon from the glory of that light
His flickering torch he must ignite.

The quiet waters soothe the soul,
Beyond, he views the final goal.
Filled with the beauty of that place,
Restored, he knows he's won the race.

SUNSHINE AND THOUGHTS

THERE is a land where fleeting thought
    forgets
Strife's unkind words and bitter, cruel deeds,
    Dreams how the glorious sunshine never
      sets,
But heals the wounded heart that frets and
    bleeds.

    Then gather up this sunshine's merry
      ray
To store where lovely things should ever be,
    And keep it safe through many a gloomy
      day!
In very sooth it is life's golden key.

THE FORGE OF LIFE

ONE poppy lies upon the open page,
Its mute dismembered petals mark in red
A passage where its vivid life was shed:
The hand that plucked the bloom on Flan-
    ders' Plain

Is stilled, and lips no longer smile and
    kiss
The petals in the glaring sunset glow
Of Vimy Ridge; as all the world may know
You both have shared the victor's crown
    of life.

But men must mourn a hero's early grave,
While women softly whisper: "Peace is best:
Beneath the scarlet poppies they shall rest,
Whose life-blood ebbed away on Flanders'
    Plain."

If flaming swords that turn each way and
    twist
Between the living and the sleeping dead
Stand guard with poppy blooms of vivid red
Around the monument on Vimy Ridge,

And bring a lasting peace to mark the page
For valiant souls who for a space must pause,
They have not kept the faith in vain because
Death's victory encircles Vimy Ridge.

THE OTTAWA WAR MEMORIAL

WRAPPED in the silence of a starry night,
Freedom, above the drums of battle din,
Linking her force with her great sister,
    Peace,
Claims the brave souls who strove her cause
    to win.

Living again through sculpture's magic art,
Blending their voices in the mystic dream,
Hearts throb in unison with heavenly
    spheres:
Honour with Peace is woven in the scheme.

4

THE NATIONAL WAR MEMORIAL

CROWNING a monument of cold grey stone,
Freedom and Peace their glorious forms
 enthrone,
Keeping a vigil through the silent night,
Pleading for those who, after bitter strife,
Have, with their unsheathed swords, for
 victory, life.

Designed and moulded with the sculptor's
 art,
Life dawns again, and each brave throbbing
 heart
Cries out to every careless passer-by,
"Heed, heed! We fell in Freedom's sacred
 cause."
Peace, bending, crowns her sister with ap-
 plause.

Swords drawn for Peace have fanned the
 fiercest flame,
Leaving the wounded souls, the blind, the
 lame,
Groping through life for love that must
 inspire
To higher deeds than cruel hellish hate,
Poured like a vial of wrath and desolate.

Thronging the monument winged souls take
  shape,
Seeking from sordid turmoil swift escape,
Vast surging numbers swell the advancing
  host,
Eagerly entering unknown paths of light,
Eyes dare not follow this immortal flight.

A CAROL

WE search a world mad cruel and wild
As once three Magi sought the Child,
To pray the Christ, the Prince of Peace,
That wars through Him forever cease.

The Wisemen seek His peace afar
But strifes befall, their quest to mar:
They beg a Star to guide the way
Lest men sink low in sin this day.

While quiring angels sing on high,
And shepherds herding flocks reply,
His Star shines down with heavenly light,
And holy fears enwrap the night.

Then straight the trees with blossoms new
Attire in majesty to view,
And every star with candle bright
Brings joy to those three Wisemen's sight.

TO A TEA-POT

LITTLE brown pot with handle and spout,
Many a time you have helped me out
With cheering brew that's good to sup,
When day is done and I sum it up.

Your spout has a chip on the very tip,
Recalling the hour when I let you slip,
You did not shatter and I was glad,
Losing you would have made me sad!

A friend in need is a friend indeed,
You are a friend with your fragrant weed,
To drink and dream and snooze away
After the work of a well-worn day.

THE HEART OF EMPIRE
(1937)

A LITTLE Isle, that spans the seven seas,
Is pulsing with the history of past years,
Toward which the sentiment of Empire
turns.
We watch thy unfolding triumphs once
again,
In welding destinies in a long chain
Of sovereigns—kings and queens and em-
perors!
Your princes, nobles, men of great renown
Are gathering East and West to swell the
van.
From the Dominions come first ministers,
From India come the princes, great with
gold
And jewelled trains, with loyalty and pride.
South Africa is mustering a band
Of statesmen proud of Dutch and British
blood,
Erst foes, now friends in a free Common-
wealth.
Australians, foremost with their men of
might,
Arrive, strong, bronzed and keen, with loyal
hearts,

To take their places in this pageantry.
New Zealanders have joined the race to meet
The parent stock of lineage, tried and true;
And, intermingling French and British blood
With alien peoples in joint homage bound,
The choice of Canada will greet her King—
All knit by bonds unsevered yet through
    feud.
And Erin's sons come, too, from North and
    South,
To view the King's anointing—ancient rites
Beside the mystic stone, where Jacob slept
Of old, and made his covenant with God.
This earthly power is pledge to safeguard
    home
And subjects' rights beyond the Seven Seas.
So may God save Their Majesties, and grant
Them health and wealth, to sway the scep-
    tered throne
For justice, peace, prosperity and weal
To all who dwell beneath our Empire's flag!

HARMONY OR DISCORD?

AWAKE, wronged soul, awake and live again!
The universe is lovely past desire,
The world has all it needs for happiness,
So prize a world of light that keeps men
    sane!

Why strengthen barriers of gloom, aware
That iron bars will shut out wholesome
    light?
Have you no dream for life's high destiny?
This is not freedom: it is blank despair.

Destructive wars must cease with raging
    fires
Of hate and gaping wounds that foul the air,
Entraining in their sickening wake a swarm
Of plagues, that slough men in most
    wretched mires

Of tortures life destroyed may never slake.
With ineradicable blots they smear
The soul, and cloud the sun in heaven's
    vault.
They dull and deafen all that joys might
    wake

Transcendent everywhere in Nature's
    moods,
Pure wonder cadences of melody,
Which all Creation sings in harmony,
Essential as the sweets of earthly foods.

Arise at morn to greet rose-tinted beams,
And seize and hold the glory of a day!
For none may steal the rapture that unfolds
These fine impenetrating early gleams.

Why discords, strifes, disease, and filth,
    and war?
Fair Nature's marvels form a barrier set
In tranquil loveliness, enveloping
Its tenants, lest one sorry speck might mar

The dawn's approach, the world's most
    gladdening song
That pours from every pulsing, thankful
    throat,
The fragrancy of earth at sunset's close,
In ever tuneful phrasing, growing strong.

The strains of harmonies throughout the
    nights,
The music of the spheres which all may hear,

Revive the soul, the conqueror of fate,
And leave no discords sounding on the
heights.

The mountains, rivers, forests, plains and
seas
Combine in unison of fuller life,
Absorbing rays lent by a sun's vast
strength.
Why blot out these with doleful miseries?

Encompassed in the sunshine of the soul
Man is no puppet in a game of chance,
For each has his appointed work to do,
And, doing, adds his unit to the whole.

VISIONS OF A WOUNDED SOUL

Would Life might give me back my blood
    and youth,
Strong to achieve, ere blighting war had
    spent
The nations in an agonizing death,
Or left but raw and festering wounds, that
    rent

The very soul dragged down to blank des-
    pair.
Where are the fields of France with poppies
    red?
Where all the tumult, glorious acclaim
Of heroes, who in Freedom's cause had bled?

Why linger we so maimed, distraught and
    blind,
Helpless, confined as in a prisoner's cell?
And yet these self-same poppies by the door
Give pause to doubt: in varied hues they
    tell

Of changed adventure in a foreign land,
Where e'en the poppy rises like a rose
In double beauty, hue and perfect form,
Or as a fringed chrysanthemum would pose.

The poppy's red is merging with the years,
As dreams of youths who gird themselves
    to slay
Are left behind with pillage, hate, revenge,
And monuments in stone or common clay.

Beyond this chaos, an "awful rose of dawn"
Bridges a path where friends and foes are
    free,
And wounded souls may find the quest they
    sought
With poppies waving on the upward lea.

BUDDIES

"It's jolly Dick," I heard 'im say,
So close we lay that peppy day,
We was a-lyin' in the trench
When come that shell.   O Lord, the wrench!

Well, 'ee was took.   I've carried on
In Christie Street for twenty year.
Poor chap!   I wonder where 'ee's gone.
Last night I thought 'ee walked in 'ere.

'Ee caught my hand and held it hard.
"We done our bit out there, we two."
Ay Dick, you took the parting card,
So quick you went, my buddy true.

I've lingered on for twenty year.
Who got the best of it, and why?
My legs went first.   Now, ain't that queer?
Don't ask me mo' or I might lie.

Dick, come again!   The night's not long
When you blow in so brave and strong.
Just hold my hand as 'ow you've done:
The march, old friend, has just begun.

JOY BELLS IN WAR-TIME

WHERE may Christmas refuge find
In a world dipt red in gore?
Once she fled great Herod's wrath,
And her star shines as of yore.

When the shepherds sore afraid
Viewed with awe its questing light,
Bleeding hearts and anguished souls
Hailed its wonder with delight.

Softening grief, a spirit guide
Carols music, clear and bold,
Warning Earth to heed the call
Heaven's scroll has now unrolled.

Infant weal and Christmas mirth
Cheer mankind with healing wings,
Joy bells ring out "Love and Peace"
Through war's din, while Nature sings.

A SONG OF CHOPIN

Despite his many foes and feeble frame,
To Chopin's soul unceasingly there came
Strange tunes his dextrous fingers woke in
    play,
Delighting duller minds of common clay.

Etudes, preludes, depicting mysteries rare,
Vague longings, yearnings in the balmy air,
Hearts with sorrows broken, dream-loves
    crushed to dust,
All earth in a tumult, armour red with rust.

New rhythms in new tempos spun their
    brilliant tunes,
Old ballades and waltzes, ancient magic
    runes,
Sunshine brightness sparkling in glittering
    drops of rain,
The polonaise, joy kindling by charm of
    music's strain.

Nocturne and berceuse, too, lulled anguished
    griefs and moans
In swelling harmonies and lingering pedal
    tones;

But unrelenting Fate sent forth his poison
    fangs,
And plagued the shrinking flesh with
    ceaseless torturous pangs.

When Genius and Love stood by on tender
    quest,
Sweet airs unheard rang in that stricken
    breast,
Whose death-bed aspirations' reveries
Still soothe poor souls on life's tumultuous
    seas.

To Chopin, master of his art, remote and
    shy,
Came melodies from mists or windy sky,
And every dainty, filmy, fleecy cloud
Seemed it alone should form his winding
    shroud.

THE INSTRUMENT

Mute strings at rest and all unstrung!
When will your music live again
To stir the inmost soul's recess
And shower vibrating chords around
A world gone mad with strain and stress?
The subtle fingers, nimbly flexed
To fit the strings and bridge in place,
Are stiff and still, and hold no more
The bow with graceful wrist and light,
To waken melodies of song.

    In other days they called forth strains
Invoked by master minds to tune
With Nature's dark or merry moods:
Deep tones recalling surging seas,
Or storms of lightning, winds and rain,
And sudden soughings, changes swift
To low, clear harmonies that breathed
Of fragrant fields and singing birds,
Of zephyr breezes, fanning isles
Untorn by agonies of war.

    They move a yearning in the soul
To leave the artificial, false,
And roam again in beauty's bower,
To drink the pure sweet rills of mirth,
A draught to drain most lovingly.
Full many an outraged mind they soothed,

And led to havens yet unknown.
     Our brains are instruments in tune
With Time and Space, rekindling love
As tribute to the Lord of All,
Who dowered the body, freed the soul
Ordained to weave its destiny.
O glorious Spirit, impulse blest
To rouse a thousand memories
And send the anguished wounded soul,
By tortures riven, one moment's ease
From Satan's fell device to gain
The mastery! You lift the veil
That shrouds the noblest gift from Heaven
So all may glimpse the love unseen,
Sustaining life with muted strings,
Where man on his triumphal quest
May sing successive harmonies,
Upborne on Nature's airy wings.

MELODIES

HEAR you not the breeze with melodies
Whisper softly to the ancient trees?
Nature in her twilight hours of rest
Loves Apollo's tuneful lyre the best.

THE MOONLIGHT SONATA

THE Master wove in melodies
A people's songs borne on the breeze,
While every tender, soft moonbeam
In beauty rounded out his dream.

His ears had loved each tuneful note
That filled the happy warbler's throat,
With them he blent in sweet refrain
A masterpiece to soothe his pain.

When deaf to outward harmonies
His soul's sonata brought him ease,
Thus Nature aids with fond caress
Her favourite sons in their distress.

Great God of battles for the brave,
Grant man the will to seek and save
The race from cruel miseries
That change great joys to bitter lees!

Let music sound between the nodes
To lift the mind's despairing loads!
Beethoven, stricken, found the fires
His soul had sought with wild desires.

SECRET OF A TUNE

"DARLING little piper man,
Tell me, an it please you can,
Where you find each merry tune
Ere the sun has reached high noon!"

"Winsome maiden as you pass,
Listen to the blades of grass,
As you trip and lightly go,
Ask them all you wish to know."

"Why! the blades of grass say naught.
I've passed oft, but no sound caught
Where they spring a vivid green
Round my paths and in between."

"Hiding there, I find my tune
Ere the sun has reached high noon.
Growth's the very breath of Spring,
Nature cannot help but sing."

THE MYSTERY OF MUSIC

When Schubert caught his melodies
Adrift in space on airy wings,
He drew sweet music from the spheres
To quicken every phrase Earth sings.

He found the harp Aeolus played
In thunder clouds and pattering rains,
In forest storms and ocean surge,
And set their rhythms to his strains.

A wanderer in Elysian fields,
He heard immortal symphonies,
The fugitives of heart's desire,
Romance and love and harmonies.

These mingled with the mystic fires
Hephaestus guards eternally,
Lest mortals win to Beauty's realm
And hold her in captivity.

BABY LOVE-BIRD AND HIS MISTRESS

BABY LOVE-BIRD

(*To Miss Doris Sherwood, in memory
of a delightful entertainment given by her clever
little bird on the occasion of a recent visit*)
July 2, 1941

A WONDROUS bird with plumage gay
His loving mistress brought one day,
To cheer the sick and sip some tea
And revel with sweet revelry.

On each neck feather, small and white,
Lies one black pearl, a lovely sight,
And snowy as his necklaced throat
Are cap and face and petticoat.

A fringe of dark blue on the last
Peeps shyly as he hurtles past,
His breast puffs out with rarest blues,
Sky tints and aqua's limpid hues.

Round dark quick eyes, fine claws like
    hands,
Small ears that catch all kind commands,
Swift wing-spread strong for flight and bold
With shimmering tail mark heirlooms old.

The marvel grew as words he sang:
In human speech new love tones rang,
And whispered nothings from his beak
Now proved how sweetly birds can speak.

The charming creature showed no fright
As on strange shoulders he would light
And tell the tales of other lands,
Where Paradise blooms on the sands.

Away beyond the sea, his mates
Share all the joys that God creates,
His forests, orchids, fruits far famed,
"We budgerigars are aptly named."

Farewell, sweet love-bird, in thy wake
Deep thoughts arise, the soul to shake:
Let ugly weapons hate has found
Corrode in rust on desert ground!

WOODLAND FANCIES

MOST lovely are the friendly trees
When merrymakers bask at ease,
Their foliage hides the haunts of birds
Whose songs are thanks more deep than
    words.

They find a prize in every leaf,
In scattered grain beside the sheaf,
The air the sunshine wind and rain
All help their livelihood to gain.

A fragrance from the blossomed bough
Perfumes the upturned sod and plough:
A gaily plumaged clever train
Pay homage with their sweet refrain.

Till Autumn's bleakness, far and wide,
Awakes strange instincts for their guide,
That send them winging through the night
From frosty Winter's nipping bite.

In ancient days when all were free
Great men held court beneath a tree,
The forests sang the hunter's song
Of antlered stag and quarry strong.

If man could turn from work to rest
What peace would soothe his troubled breast!
A burden's never half so light
As when it slips quite out of sight.

Work need not be a scourge of rods
To break men like unseasoned clods,
Just watch the growing tree with fruit
And note the marvel of its root!

Dame Nature's weaving silent care
Bestows rich gifts above compare,
With swift magnetic force her dream
Brings magic charm to Beauty's scheme.

As days grow short and cold winds blow,
While softly drifting falls the snow,
Hearth fires burn warm and crackle clear,
The tree's aflame to bring good cheer.

A NORMANDY MEADOW

THE sea foamed and splashed on the rocks
    far below,
  Echoing thoughts from the deep,
Herbs yielded sweet fragrance throughout
    the green meadow,
  Wherein the hare had her keep.

The heart beat in tune to this scene of repose,
  Praising the heavens so gay,
Where the swift changing blues and the light
    winds and sunshine
  Danced to gladden the day.

The larks fluttered up, then more swiftly
    arose,
  Outspreading their wings like sails,
Their songs caught the lilt of the voice in
    the grasses
  When soaring above the dales.

A hush lulled the meadow as twilight des-
    cended,
  The chalice of Nature was filled
With fragrance and bird song and beauty
    commingled,
  In sunshine and wind song distilled.

MYOSOTIS

Myosotis in a garden grew
So modestly and prettily,
Some children passed, who heedlessly
Plucked up the plants to throw away.

"Must all our charms lie wasted here,
Where blind feet trample ruthlessly
The life He gave so tenderly?"
There passed a youth who dreamed that
    day.

Among the trees and bushes fair,
He saw their plight, and skilfully
Replaced the flowers lovingly.
This happened in the month of May.

FIRST BUDS

He brought me willows brown and sweet,
Along their stems white gleams of light,
Wakening with Spring's returning feet
To spy earth's coverlet of snow.

The day before warmed by the sun
Shook free of Winter's icy grip,
And loosed snows in the wayside run,
But once more bitter winds blew cold.

The willows showed no least regret,
So firm and strong each twig stood up,
Their nurselings nestling did not fret
At March, who played them such a trick.

The world had given back life again!
With deep content they viewed the scene
Still held by chill winds' nipping pain,
And knew full well that Spring was near.

And on the threshold of his life,
Its wonder in his dreaming eyes,
Could he, I mused, escape the strife
That wrecks a world distraught with pain?

Is there no way to save youth's dream
Of beauty in the universe?
Is lovely light an empty beam,
Void of joy's message for mankind?

HARMONIES

WHEN Spring is in the air again
And fresh life wakes with purpose new,
There is a harmony that's felt,
As when sweet flowers bathe in dew.

Below earth's surface far remote,
A Being stirs with conscious love,
The sun and air breathe melody,
A whispered note as of the dove.

There is no room for hate's fierce strife,
Above, the stars gleam as of old,
Perchance their watching lights will guide
True harmonies within the fold.

Mankind exists for life and hope,
Fair earth took shape for his domain,
His brain should guard and guide and shape
Brave destinies that skill may gain.

The elements, earth sea and air,
Revolve with mixed humanity,
Each weaving in a free design,
While Fates spin fast their destiny.

SPRING'S LOOM

Hurry up, hurry up! Spring has come out!
See the new buds that are crowding about.
Nectars are spraying the air with perfume,
Spring weaves a winsome world fresh on her
    loom.

Lilt of gay laughter and bright smiling eyes
Waken with sweetness at every surprise,
Hill slopes and valleys are turning to green,
Rippling, the rivulets gurgle between.

Hurry up, hurry up! Trip it along!
Dancing to Nature's new, wonderful song,
Bird life and flowers and lovers will woo,
Spring whispers softly "Dear love, I love
    you!"

CARAGANA FLOWERS

AMID the caragana's golden blooms
The humming-birds are sipping in delight
And fanning drowsy air with whirring wings,
Their colours flashing, glowing gems of life.
Etherial and beautiful this scene,
Like harmonies of paradisal bliss,
The ecstasy, the rapture and the thrill,
A festival of humming-birds and blooms.

THE GUEST

THE seeking soul has found the path of light
That guides us onward to the open gate,
Where, warm, the hand of friendship clasps
    our own,
And love has vanquished all the bitter night.

Ah, glorious guest of love, that makes life
    bright,
Strew thy rich gifts around us ere we go!
This universe is lovely past desire,
Awake and prize what gives such great
    delight!

Greet dawn's approach, its pleasures new
    and strange
May fill the heart with raptures never
    known,
Till light has flooded all the soul with joy,
And in its growing strength we see the
    change.

From Earth to Heaven the pilgrim finds
    his way
In one swift flash, and many a weary mile
Behind him lies, his song is wild and free,
The sunshine of the soul makes glad the
    day.

Good-bye to sorrows, hopelessness and fear!
For every day will bring its glad tomorrow.
With darkness banished from the spirit
    sphere,
There is no gloom, no doubt, throughout
    the year.

THE LIGHT OF THE WORLD

THE sprites of the Winter were building a
    scene,
And they merrily hung tiny bells,
That tinkled with frost as the wind blew a
    tune,
"The birds' cradle song," say the mothers
    who croon
By their little ones' cots as the Yuletide
    draws near,
When grim hate is vanquished by love and
    good cheer.
    "Feed my lambs," the Master said,
    "And see! The feast is duly spread."

Each mother will offer a prayer tonight,
As into her heart there will steal
A feeling of comfort, her children are dear
And her joy rings a note that is hopeful and
    clear.
The love of an infant so tenderly true
Drives sorrow and strife from the earth
    made anew.
    "Let the little ones come," hear Him say,
    "To God's kingdom belong such as they."

At Christmas in many a land is retold
How wise men once followed a star,
To seek for a babe to be born on that night,
And how shepherds at watch were sore in
affright
When a new star appeared as they herded
their sheep,
Unseen by the rest of mankind sunk in sleep.

"I am the Light of the whole world wide,
Hold ye fast to my love that my peace may
abide!"

ILLUSIONS

By noon the trees are robed in shimmering
    snow,
Like diamonds sparkling 'neath the sun's
    bright ray,
Yet frost-encircling crystals there they stay.
By night, the moon's soft beams' enchanting
    glow
Delights the earth-born who forget their
    woe
Recalling mythic tales that old folks say
Of fairyland, where elves and goblins play.
Aye, who are they who Nature's secrets
    know!
   Through silent nights, safe hid from hu-
    man eye,
Her artists wrought with magic brush and
    pen
To change the landscape, moor and sea and
    fen,
Yet still elude our grasp howe'er we try.
Are they the toilworn, idle dreams of men,
Or does their beauty show that God is nigh?

THE SPIRIT OF CHRISTMAS

THE city is laved in the moonlight's soft
    hues,
And in woods every stately majestical tree
Stands gossamer white in the frosts spun
    from dews,
While Nature broods hushed in expectancy.

The glorious calm of this wondrous midnight
Is stirred by the chimes from the carillon
    tower,
As Christmas appears in a maze of delight
On the stroke of that mystical, magical hour.

Sweet Spirit who wingest to earth once again,
Thy fane has been raised by the Infinite
    Hands;
To roam in such beauty a Christ-Child
    might deign,
Where outlined in arches and splendours it
    stands.

Each delicate tracery's garlanded spray
Confesses the Presence to woodland in
    prayer,
Clad in vesture surpassing the noblest array
E'er fashioned by man with most exquisite
    care.

The breezes are cadenced in song as they
    blow,
A people are offering their love to the Child,
The waters are chilled in the race of their
    flow,
Once again shall Peace dawn, with a vision
    beguiled.

SAINT PATRICK

Saint Patrick came to Ireland
To give the folks a helping hand.
"This little leaf is one yet three,
An emblem of the Trinity,"

He said, and picked the greenest blade
That grows so modest in the shade.
Thus Patrick showed as all might see
The shamrock shared a trinity.

And Erin's folk adored the Saint
Who taught them tales so old and quaint:
He even charmed the snakes away
Because they feared his stinging lay.

The devil bit the rocks with rage,
His cunning could not oust the sage,
He fled the Isle for other spheres,
Where soon the streets were filled with biers.

In many a spot are shown his stills
Around the gorse clad Wicklow Hills,
Where that Ould Boy with moonshine brew
Consoled the demons of his crew.

The divil, indade, Saint Pat would curse
If he should make Old Erin worse
Than other lands where'er you turn
With famine and feuds and flames that
burn.

A SEPTEMBER GARDEN

My garden, well prepared in Spring,
Alack, has gone a-rollicking,
'Tis true, production did not fail
For many seeds were sent air-mail.

They're not the seeds were planted here:
It's all mysterious and queer.
Perhaps the birds' to-whit, to-woo
May tell the secret when they coo.

It should have been a lovely plot,
Instead the place has gone to pot,
A rakish growth, flowers, weeds and grass,
That sprang to life a tangled mass.

Thus is the garden of mankind
Upset by every changing wind:
In Eden, folks rejoiced in Spring,
Then after went a-rollicking.

THE DANDELION

WHEN dandelions start to grow
And change the fields to living gold,
It seems as if the sun's bright glow
Is caught by fairy hands, that hold

And weave their heads in one bright gleam
To flash across the greening lea
And banks beside the rippling stream,
A strange sweet mystery to see.

For suddenly, as light as air,
They wave before our wondering eyes
White puffs that sail without a care:
The dandelion never dies.

It's all so wonderfully done.
Just watch the wind's aerial play!
Why not join in the merry fun,
While dandelions float away.

THE LILY OF THE VALLEY

THE lily of the valley
Is drifting through the fragrant vale,
And meets in snowy loveliness
The fury of the gale.

But morning finds her ringing
Her low sweet bells for woodland prayer,
The florets listen eagerly
For life is smiling there.

THE ARTIST AUTUMN

THE artist Autumn blows a madcap gale,
And trembling Summer leaves the fragrant
    vale:
She mourns her dying flower and falling leaf
And dubs the artist chap a sorry thief,

Whose hostile brush takes her own work
    away.
This artist fellow with his colours gay
Paints all the hills a flaming dance of gold,
While starry frosty nights are growing cold.

Hot Summer's sun sends down a healthy ray
To warm the vivid asters through the day,
The maples wave their flags of crimson
    thread
That lightly flutter to a cosy bed.

Earth's spinning cycles bring evolving
    change,
Each season ushers in the new and strange,
Frail beauties fade in Autumn's waning
    light,
Dawn brings fresh charms to captivate the
    sight.

OUR GOODLY HERITAGE

YEA, friend, we have a goodly heritage,
A nestling lodge among the wooded hills
When silver lights play through the spark-
    ling rills
And Fall shades tint each burnished brilliant
    page.

Soft cover they for Summer blooms just
    slain,
Yet there speaks naught of unreturning
    Spring,
A Winter's sleep will soothe their airy wing.
O, Fall, thy feet are lovely on the plain!

New beauties stir the soul's inmost recess,
The coloured fragrant fruits, the laden trees,
The hush of birds, the herds, the drowsy bees,
And Nature revelling in her loveliness.

Through Beauty's realm the soul may soar
    in flight,
And there amid the mysteries of life
Behold "The Song Celestial" quelling strife:
The whole round world is flooded with its
    light.

What if Fall yield to Winter once again,
So memories live, awakening thoughts that
    run
And add their quota to each hour begun,
Recalling dancing feet across the plain.

Great Sagittarius guards with ready bow,
And Heaven greets Earth to tend her broken
    soil,
When man may aid with thoughtful, well
    planned toil,
If toil it be to quell each deadly foe.

The lodge is shaded by a crimson tree,
And in the orchard stands the cider press,
None know the poignant stab of cold and
    stress,
Each one may sup in sweet tranquillity.

Then through the portals floats a song un-
    known,
The mists on mountain tops merge in the
    sky,
And dark cool pools hold mirrored stars on
    high
While Fall in many tones chaunts "Sum-
    mer's flown."

LEAVES ASTIR

YE leaves now soft astir within the sap
That swelling fills the boughs so soon to bud
Your rustlings thrill with melodies of Spring,
Bestowing gifts to cast in Nature's lap.

Tradition's glorious spinning merges song
Of warbling birds and woodland's bursting
    dawn,
For Winter's reign of ice is passing now,
And all things wake to life, and bear along

Creation's rustling burthen toward new
    light,
Which upward, outward, thrusts, to seek
    the crest
And greet the sun-warmed fragrancy of
    earth
That turns with vernal urge from drowsy
    night.

Ye greening blades that throb with large
    increase,
Ye timid shy things lurking in the shades,
Ye fish and fowl returning from your haunts,
Ye racing waters wild with your release

Behold fair Nature's rhythmical accord
With harmonies which guard her secrecies,
While dormant potencies with magic wings
Secure this freedom's mystical reward.

A POT OF LAVENDER

ACCEPT this plant of lavender
With silvery leaves of fragrance rare,
That shyly peeped from seeds last spring.
It may survive the frosts with care.

Of other days it speaks to me,
When grandma in the minuet
Was hooped and looped so properly:
She never did a pirouette!

It's all new-fangled dance today,
The tangos foxtrots dips and glides,
A flight in aeroplane or car,
And cigarettes dished up besides.

Old-fashioned? Yes it may be, still
Attractive as sweet Watteau maids
At rest with harp in fairy scenes,
With love and song in sylvan glades.

Yet in those days of daintiness
Our heroines were splendid dames,
Reserved and true and brave withal,
They kept men great with noble aims.

Would we might call old-fashioned, too,
War's fever with its many ills
That plague the world! 'Twere better far
Attired in jabots lace and frills.

Then come buy lavenders, kind sir!
They'll mind you of a summer's day
When joyous youth to Mitcham rode.
Kind sir, will you not take a spray?

THE WINDOW BOX

DELICATE lobelia
Nodding from your green box,
Greeting passers-by,

Waving your fresh colours,
Blues that vie with heaven,
For the maid that tends you!

Lo, now! Broken-hearted,
Ghostlike on your frail stems
Droop the tender flowerets.

Maid, why lavish loving,
If to leave them pining
You must haste away?

WINTER'S HERALD

I AM coming from the Spirit World,
Through the wind and rain,
Hearken to my pleading,
People now are needing
Comforts for today.

I am coming from the Spirit World,
Breezes chill and keen
Whisper in their blowing,
Those of us well knowing
List to what they say.

I am coming from the Spirit World,
My grip is icy cold,
Long days now are waning,
The seasons ever gaining
Whisper, "No delay!"

I am coming from the Spirit World,
Wisdom points the way,
Sleep is now caressing
Earth in Winter dressing,
Nature's peace holds sway.

APRIL SNOWS

WHERE is April hiding now
All her tears and laughter?
Will she cheer us on our way
Now and then and after?

What has she to do with snow,
Frosts and cold winds sighing?
Harbinger of dainty Spring,
See, new buds are dying!

Hasten with sweet sunlit breeze,
Set the woodland thrilling
In a dance of colours gay
To the warblers' trilling!

A SONG FOR TODAY

(May, 1937)

THE snows melt at last,
   A plough turns the sod,
The first greens peep through,
   A bird's on the bough,
The worm comes out now,
   And earth's soaked with dew.
The sun smiles like God,
   All's well, Winter's past.

THE SOURCE

DEEP in a virgin forest basked a lake,
A spotless mirror when the air was still,
Giving its pure fresh waters lavishly,
That wood-folk unafraid might drink their
    fill.

Beneath its placid depths unheard, unseen,
Its source, a living spring, forever flowed,
The untainted substance of our Mother
    Earth,
For all her children's weal in love bestowed.

Here came rapacious men, who for quick
    gain
Laid low the trees a hungry mill to feed,
That poured into the lake its poisonous
    waste,
Till all life vanished, victims of their greed.

Yet still, sweet water bubbled from the
    earth,
Pure as of old, awaiting better days
When horrid filth shall cease, no more to
    choke
The pulsing life fulfilling Nature's ways.

At last the forest perished utterly,
When man, the arch destroyer, had worked
      his will;
Gone were the lordly trees, till none remained
To feed the silent, now dismantled mill.

Thus fierce destructive forces everywhere
Batten, like Saturn, on their own foul brood,
For evil ever bears the seeds of death
And soon or late must yield its place to good.

Up welled the spring, and through its gentle
      might
Prevailed against the foetid noisomeness,
Filling the lake anew with sustenance,
Till joyous life returned, its gifts to bless.

Fret not because our world is stained with
      crime,
Blind hates, unbridled lusts in many a land,
For underneath still flows Eternal Love,
To compass all when once men understand.

WHERE THE PAST LINGERS

Once childish laughter kept this house aglow,
But now lurks emptiness, above, below.
Where are the flowers that made the plot
    so gay?
Where those green shoots to sprout another
    day?

The mother hand so happy in her toil
Lies silent in the grave, untouched the soil,
Far from the silent home the brood has
    flown,
No merry chatter wakes the land unsown.

The house once filled with energy and love
Is still, and still the stormy winds above
The apple orchard with no bloom in sight,
The cedar hedge unclipt, while men-folk
    fight.

Decay shows here and there from roof to
    floor,
Slow turns the old key in the creaking door
'Twixt hearth where now no crackling pine-
    logs burn
And window where still waits the idle churn.

Deserted now and lonely past recall
The old house shivers; in its silent hall
Perhaps there hovers still the shade of one
Who laid her burden down when work was
    done.

A mother's imprint plainly lingers here,
Whole worlds are peopled by a love so dear,
And hearts that for their broods so freely
    gave
Their all in all still beat beyond the grave.

ODE
TO THE GATINEAU RIVER

SWIFT child of northern springs that dwell
    below
Earth's surface, whence a secret nurture
    brought
Your tiny drops to warmth and sunlight's
    glow,
On Nature's mission tirelessly you've
    wrought.

The ancient hills that knew your infant days
O'er all your windings keep their vigils still,
And by your stream the blue flag lightly
    sways,
While o'er you floats the song of whip-poor-
    will.

A lonesome trail you lay, when cold winds
    swept
And teams paced back and forth with winter
    loads,
Asleep in snow and ice where shy things
    crept,
Your race delayed along the frozen roads.

You woke in spring, when every freshet bore
As gift abounding life, and March storms
     loud
Sped on toward ocean with a mighty roar,
While sunlit air rolled up your misty cloud.

You gathered strength from every rill around
To join your sisters in their high flood tide,
And rushed in heedless headlong fury,
     bound
For some far goal unknown save to your
     guide.

You rocked frail crafts and tossed them
     back, and flashed
Your white-caps on the air with merry glee,
You played a joyous game of foam, and
     splashed
And caught each heavy burden carelessly.

In tumult over rocks you leapt, and whirled
The logs amid the foam to churn and seethe,
While on your banks the silver birch un-
     furled
Her leaves for garlands o'er your spray to
     wreathe.

But now, great walls of stone confine your
course,
For man has curbed your might to work his
will,
And bound to servile wheel your torrent
force
For genie's tasks in home and busy mill.

In days gone by, you never charmed as when
We strolled through woods, and watched
you flowing nigh,
Or tented on your flowered slopes—ah, then,
Dear Gatineau, 'twas hard to say good-bye!

THE ARCANA OF NATURE

CAN we learn all this old world knows?
Festive May shows with gleams of light
Orchards blooming, rose-pink and white,
Nature's workshop in sweet repose.

Scattered soon are the blossoms rare
Leaving delicate fruits in green,
Modest violets peep between
Sedums covering rocks stript bare.

Dainty shading is everywhere,
Freighted cargoes too rich to hold
Wrapt in petals are now unrolled,
Spreading beauty beyond compare.

Aeons pass while the mystery,
Knowledge herself, profoundly deep,
Lies within her most ancient keep,
Time alone guards the master key.

MYSTIC JEWELS

THAT night, the city lights just twinkled
    twice,
As greeting from a pilgrim hurrying past,
Then flashed His lightnings round the house
    and grounds.
His thunders rolled in awful tones and deep,
And every man and bird and beast fled fast
To cover, when a storm of rain and hail
Came down and chained roads trees and
    fields with frost,
And overhead formed clinging icicles
Festooning eaves and branches, walls and
    wires.
All through the night His signals flashed,
    until
Dawn broke o'er that transparent glassy sea,
While Earth stayed breathless in an icy grip.
The sun in sudden splendour through the
    clouds
Enmeshed the scene in flaming, flashing
    rays,
Swiftly transforming silver lights to gold,
To jasper and sardonyx, and the twelve
Great precious stones that garnish Heaven's
    walls,

Guarded by gates of pearl, through which
        the soul
May pass and see her God.   No mortal eye
Dare view the sea of glass, where mingling
        fires
Burnish the jewels of His realm, the souls
That seek life's higher paths to wisdom,
        truth
And beauty, and the love that hath no price.

MY PRESCRIPTION

So, when you're tired of the books,
Take but a day to follow joy,
Go seek the babbling of the brooks,
And in the woods your time employ!

For Nature does not lack a cure,
Her secret there doth work like leaven
On mind diseased by city lure,
Until the contrast seems like Heaven.

To heal the mind and body too,
For that and mind are two in one,
Strait seek repose and Nature woo,
A god's decree, when work is done.

THE TENT DWELLER

'TIS here beneath a shady tree
I pitch my tent for brief repose,
Let every leaflet stand on guard
To shield those sunbeam swords from me!

When evening falls the breezes fan,
My fevered brow is soothed at last,
The twilight hush reveals a God,
Beyond the mists, Who speaks to man.

Among the vasts the ages tell
A tale that lifts the heart from earth:
The twinkling stars, the sun, the moon
Just whisper softly: "All is well."

There is no house built with such ease
As yonder grape-vine green and lush,
It offers shade and vintage rare,
A loving-cup to soothe and please.

Then in the forest dim I'll lie,
And ponder why no house can give
The comfort ease and sweet repose
That rest me here without a sigh.

SONG OF HOPE

FROM my wide open window this sight I
    have seen:
A child, life in flower, the earth at the spring,
The trees newly clad in their foliage green,
A bird full of joy his sweet canticle sing.

With eyes partly closed, from the child's
    lips there flow
A boisterous chorus and silvery strain,
While a radiant joy sets his face all aglow,
As if from an angel he caught the refrain.

And I have felt rise from the peaceable scene
The hopes that with courage our frail hearts
    impress,
That make a blue sky where pain's darkness
    has been
And scatter their infinite dream's loveliness.

Oh, why should you weep when the world is
    so bright?
Re-awaken your childhood, and sing o'er
    and o'er
A hymn for the beauty that brings fresh
    delight,
And caress with the birds the sweet roses
    once more!

For life is a springtime that fosters the seeds
Of summer's warm moisture, so fragrant and
      soft.
Let God be the goal of your longings and
      needs,
And march on with bold eye and head held
      aloft!

THRUSHES

Through the tanglewood the thrushes trip
    As brown as any clod,
But in their spotted throats are hung
    The vesper bells of God.

And I know little secret truths,
    And hidden things of good,
Since I have heard the thrushes sing
    At dusk in Tanglewood.

DIPPERS' INN

BELOW the steps is a dipping well,
And into its waters the dipper fell,
It lay there sparkling on frosty nights,
A dream of Heaven's glowing lights.

The maiden thought they should drink it up,
The youth replied: "It's a magic cup";
Just then they heard a marriage bell
Ring tinkling down the darkening dell.

The youth made haste to say his vow,
For here was Heaven, he thought, and now
Young folk around are never loth
To come by night and plight their troth.

For stars in wells mean heavenly love,
They shower blessings from above,
And tales a-many old folk spin
Beside the steps of Dippers' Inn.

THE EMIGRANT

"As I gazed from my window at old Sugar-
    loaf,
    Sure a lump rose and stifled a tear
When the green mountain beckoned: 'Hie
    hither, my son.'
    I must go, mother mine, never fear."

Over Wicklow Hills flourished the heather
    and gorse,
    And their fragrance just filled the whole
    air,
Then his soul soared aloft in the maze of it
    all,
    As he bathed in the splendours so rare.

'Twas a fairy feast fit for a monarch to sup,
    As the turbulent sea danced and sang,
Little larks winging upward from nests hid-
    den well,
    Ah! The emigrant's heart held no pang.

Sure, it's Erin herself is an emerald isle,
    And her mountains though low are
    supreme,
With her sunshine and breezes and showers
    galore
    She has beauty as fair as a dream.

Oh, the emigrant danced in the light of the
moon,
And men said as they watched his
return,
"He has supped with the fay, she'll bewitch
him right soon,
Sure the heart of him now it will burn."

Since then legends have spread through the
whole countryside,
How the emigrant sought for a heart
Lost on Sugarloaf Hills, where the Ould Boy,
bedad,
'Twas himself bit the great stone apart.

PSYCHE

Love has to be a gentleman,
So gallant, gay and kind,
Before a simple maiden
He with bonds may bind.

Winning, lovely, true,
With curls around her face,
His Psyche flashes coyly
Darts that he may trace.

With one consent these two
Surrender to love's charms,
And life becomes a fairy-tale
To live without alarms.

ROSEMARY'S TRYST

ADOWN the fairy glen
Sweet Rosemary to seek her love
Speeds blithely on her airy wings,
And cooing, cooing, coos the dove.

With tinkling songs of glee
The bluebells waken all the dell,
And flowery zephyrs waft the news:
"She flies to greet her love," they tell.

Sweet Rosemary in tune
With sun and birds and florets gay
Coos soft, " 'Tis he, my own dear love,
Who comes to claim his Fair for aye."

YEARNINGS

NIGHT's curtain is drawn
As the moonlight's soft beam
Is lending her magic to make life a dream,
The stars call for love
From the spheres far above,
While sweet flowers sleep on the lawn.

Ah, Love of my life!
Must there ever be strife
Between warring souls here below?
Is there never a pause for true love to glow?
Must cruel winds waken and blow,
Whetting hate's murderous knife?

True love need not part:
Through the stress, storm and pain,
Ah, Love, come again, come again!
Come with the sunshine or come with the
    rain!
Love will conquer the anguish and smart,
The deeps of my soul call thy heart.

TO DUNCAN C. SCOTT
(Xmas, 1937)

Dear D.C.,
  From your book, one day,
Conning sweet passages to glean
A ripe rich harvest of rare thought
That none may ever take away,

A sudden storm from darkening skies,
O'ercast with thunder's blackest night,
Descended, blotting out the words
Which lingered, for naught living dies.

Unfolded through the harmony
And quiet skill with which you wrought,
To make the pictures live for those
Unblessed with tender melody,

Each message with its touch divine
Must centre in our universe,
"And ever mark the man apart,"
Who pours such noble sparkling wine.

The Magic House and Other Tales
Has grown a mansion full of blooms
Which twine their tendrils round the heart,
Like sunkissed flowers in woods and dales.

So thanks, my friend, for mysteries
That wake and tremble through the breast,
They banish fears oppressions glooms,
As nectar culled from memories.

For every page o'erflows with gems,
That penetrate and purify
Life's restless troubled strife with ills
The soulless fool alone condemns.

TO SIR CHARLES SAUNDERS

(This tribute from two friends appeared in the Ottawa Citizen, *on July 29, 1937, four days after his passing away)*

REMOTE in secrecy you strove
With tiny wheat germs till success
With Nature came, and growing wove
A robe to deck earth's nakedness.

Achievement's fame spread East and West,
While wonder filled the world anew,
You toiled to vanquish rust and pest
With patience like unfailing dew.

Your science brought the world's acclaim,
But we, your friends, have heard your flute
And know three muses crown your name,
Music, art, verse, your worth salute.

Unsung you shall not leave earth's spheres,
Where prairie lands in sunshine bright
Hold full corns in their golden ears,
And day's fair dawns have banished night.

F.H.E. and W.W.E.

9 781487 598288